Published by Sprout Media, LLC

ISBN-13:978-1982018559
ISBN-10:1982018550

Cover Design: Sprout Media, LLC

This title is available for special promotions, premiums, and bulk purchases. For more information, please contact Sprout Media at BizDev@GoSproutMedia.com.

Printed in the United States of America.

Marketing for Your Golf Course

How to Ace Your Marketing & Fill Up The Course

◀ OUR MANIFESTO

We believe the old way of doing things is *over*. With the advent of a mobile device in everyone's hand, we are in the midst of a once-every-50-years shift n consumption.

We believe ir doing things differently. Not to be different, but to stand out.

We freaking love brands. That can be La Croix, Exile Brewing, Red Robin, Lowry Leather, Horizon Line Coffee, or any other place that provides great experiences. A branc is what people feel. It's what they aspire to. It's who they are and what they love.

Every business has a unique story to tell. And we work to build, maintain, and expand those unique brand stories.

WHAT IS YOUR STORY?

The brands we build are setup to redefine expectations, inspire action, grow the business, and develop and cultivate long-term relationships with your clients and customers.

Our mission is to build stories that engage and brands that last.

We feel there is an incredible opportunity for golf courses -- both public and private -- to embrace digital marketing once and for all. We aren't just talking about websites, we're talking social networks, email marketing, and video, amongst other things.

MARKETING ISN'T JUST

a website ...
a Facebook page ...
a logo ...
or a brochure.

Think about it. It's a Wednesday afternoon and a group of four is trying to decide where to play golf that weekend. They have a couple local courses in mind, when one of the golfers says "I just got an email from (insert your course name) yesterday."

He quickly pulls up the email on his phone and he has a coupon waiting for him and his friends. Another golfer in the group quickly pulls up Instagram and tells the others that the course looks like it's in great shape! They all decide your course is the where they are going to book a tee time!

EVERYTHING
IS MARKETING.

This scenario can not happen unless you have an email campaign that automatically kicks out an email during the time most golfers book tee times. It also doesn't happen unless your course is very active on Instagram. Over 47% of millennials make purchase decisions based on what they see on social media.[1]

1 MARKETING 101

Marketing isn't a website.

Marketing isn't a Facebook page.

Marketing isn't a logo.

And marketing isn't a brochure.

> **MISSION**
> is what you are all about.

Marketing is all those things and so much more. It's the experience customers have. It's the promise of the brand. It's content. It's advertising. It's your staff.

Marketing is everything you do to market your business product or service.

Some of the world's best companies understand that to its core.

Take Apple for example; their company mission is:

To make a contribution to the world by making tools for the mind that advance humankind.[2]

NASA's Mission:
To pioneer the future in space exploration, scientific discovery and aeronautics research.[3]

USTA's Mission:
To promote and develop the growth of tennis.[4]

And the USGA Mission:
Promotes and conserves the true spirit of the game of golf as embodied in its ancient and honorable traditions. It acts in the best interests of the game for the continued enjoyment of those who love and play it.[5]

And now you. What is your mission? Is it to provide a great experience at local prices? To be the premier golf course in the region? Or even bigger to be a steward of the game in all ways and to provide an incredible experience any time someone comes to the course.

As a golf course, your marketing consists of everything: your staff, your photography, your videos, your website, your scorecards, your emails, your social media, your advertising ... the list goes on and on.

1 DOES DIGITAL MARKETING MATTER?

You're damn right it matters!

Before we dive into why it matters, let us ask you this question:

Do you want to be just like the radio executives who didn't believe television was here to stay?

Do you really believe digital media; websites, Facebook, Google, and text messaging aren't here to stay? And if you do believe they are here to stay, do you want your competitors to beat you there; a place where everyone is spending their time and money?

The way we consume has always been changing and evolving. It is just hard to see because we change with it.

Check out this map:

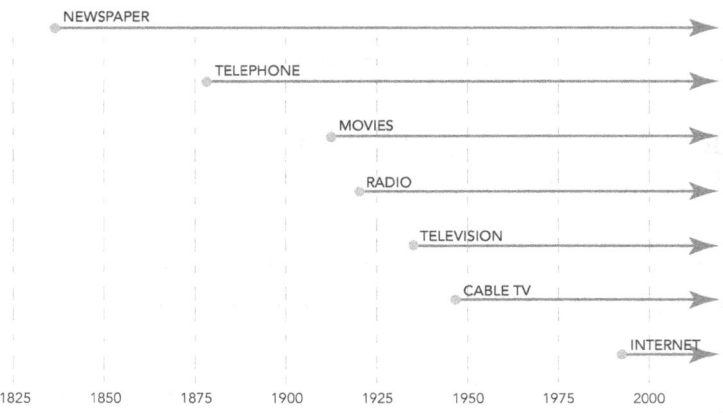

At the end of 2017, we were consuming data in vastly and dramatically different ways than even just a few years ago.

Various data sources and research studies report that adults in the United States spend between 11 and 13 hours per day with media of various types.[6] What that tells us is that adults are inundated with content throughout the day; morning, noon, and night. What that doesn't tell us is how.

The majority of users are multiple-platform users. At any given moment, users may be watching television, using their mobile device, and typing on their laptops at the same time. Our media time is no longer finite, but rather multi-dimensional, and therefore, when marketing, the strategy for any company must always be to find where the attention is; and grab it!

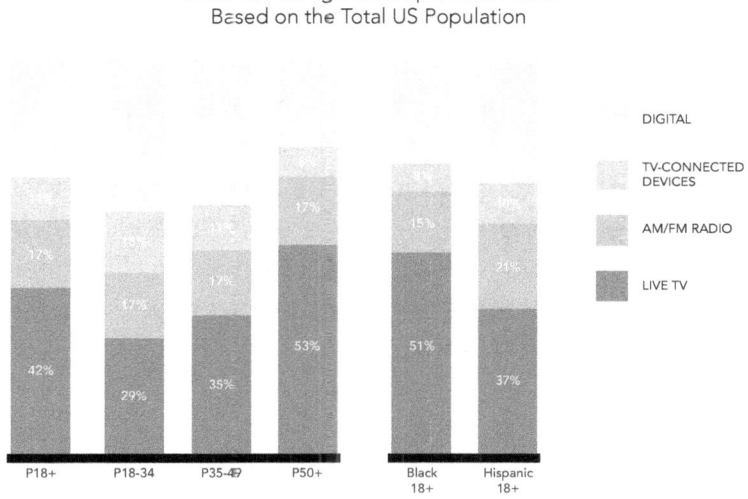

Share of Average Time Spent Per Adult
Based on the Total US Population

DIGITAL

TV-CONNECTED DEVICES

AM/FM RADIO

LIVE TV

With the rate of television consumption still around four hours a day, we still watch a significant amount of television. And that four hours amounts to nearly 33% of all media consumption in the United States; a dominant portion of all media time.

But here is the challenge with television:

Obviously our eyes are on the screen during the live action, but what happens during commercials? For a lot of viewers, that means a second screen engagement; and thus, television takes a back seat.

Merge that with the rapid rise in mobile internet use, (projected to become 26% of global media consumption in 2019)[7], and the possibilities for marketers and content producers are endless.

The youngest generation, Generation Z still watches traditional television, but not at the same level that they watch Netflix and YouTube.

Trifecta Research reports that 59%[8], or nearly six-in-ten Generation Z consumers engage with video content via "over-the-top" services, or OTT. In fact, 70% of this generation watches over two hours of YouTube content each day.

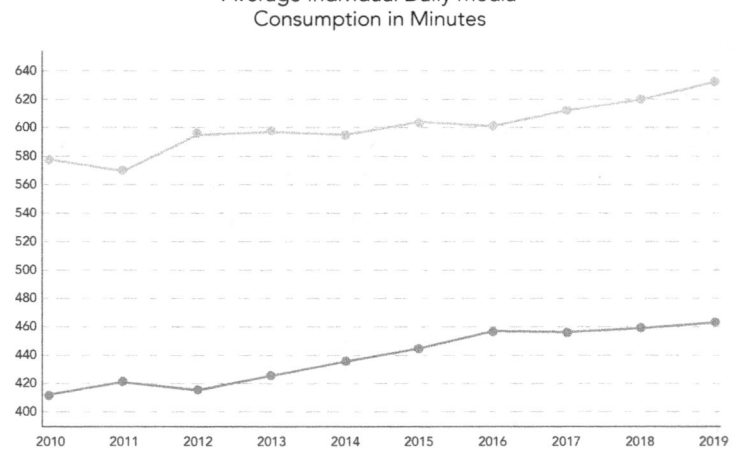

Average Individual Daily Media
Consumption in Minutes

Overall, the marketing game is all about attention and that's where a lot of agencies and companies have missed out. Attention is and always will be the key to any marketing strategy.

Just because you put up a billboard and 10,000 cars drive by every day doesn't mean that you have their attention. The same can be said for television ads, print ads, digita banner ads, and on and on.

You must always ask yourself, "Do I have their attention?" Of course, there are levels of attention and each level has a different tactic, but if you don't have their attention at the right moment, you've already lost.

◀ THE BIG 4

What does this all mean for your golf course?

While every course's strategy and tactics will vary, one thing will remain constant: Your marketing strategy must be focused on providing valuable information and content on the right platforms, in the right format, and at the right moment.

Attention is the scarce commodity that will connect the Big 4 elements together. The overall objective is to keep visitors returning for more of your content and then to frequent your course.

How exactly do you do that? By following the Big 4 of golf course marketing.

WEBSITE

First and foremost, a website. We're not talking about a website just to have a website. We're talking about a website where people can click and get all the information they could ever want about your golf course. A calendar, the ability to book a tee time, signing up for your email list, and helping visitors find your course on social media.

Your website should be where you "drive" all of your customers. A place to communicate with every single one of your customers about your course, your food and drinks, and reinforce and remind them why they should play your course!

It's 2017, everyone has a website. The small businesses, companies, and in your case, golf courses that really stand out have bright, user friendly websites; mobile too!

A major piece of website is their Search Engine Optimization (SEO). In layman's terms: SEO is the technology behind Google search results. There is a strategy to ensuring your website is found first among your competitors.

And that is the goal: to be the first thing golfers in your area find and think about.

SOCIAL

When we think of golf courses we think of pristine views, perfectly cut grass and strategically placed trees. All of these things bundled together and you can get some amazing pictures and videos.

Social media platforms, like Facebook, Instagram, Snapchat, and the like, are easy channels to provide fans and friends alike with incredible access to your golf course.

Just picture this for your golf course:
- Behind the scenes photos
- A golf pro showing how to make difficult putts

on the course
- A live look at the 1st tee box

All of these pieces of content are designed to engage your users; grab their attention and drive them to action.

Social content is not as simple as taking a picture and posting it. There needs to be a reason for the content. There is nothing worse than posting content for no reason when you have someone's attention, and wasting it.

EMAIL

When it comes to experiential businesses, Sprout Media believes that most businesses have yet to tap into the power of e-mail marketing. Sure, companies send updates and news, but e-mail has the power to drive business results when you least expect it.

All marketing, e-mail marketing especially is all about one simp e concept:

RIGHT MESSAGE.
RIGHT TIME.

One of the worst things marketers do with e-mail is blast. Just shoot emails as often as possible because ... eventually ... someone will bite! But that's not smart or strategic. That's just random. But marketing and sales aren't random.

The correct approach is to learn from your customers.

For example, have you ever signed up for a clothing company's mailing list after a purchase, only to be marketed to for weeks and months and years, but there is just random content in the emails. Worse yet is that the emails are still coming into your inbox at the same cadence as they did when you first signed up even though you haven't purchased anything since that first sale.

Long-gone are the days of just blasting emails to your list (even though many companies still take that approach). As you get to know your golfers, you're going to learn more about them; are they morning or afternoon golfers, do they come just one day a week or multiple. You're going to begin to understand what brings them to the course.

When you have that contextual information, that is when you can really make some magic happen in your e-mail (or text message) marketing efforts.

Here is an idea for you: You have a group of golfers who you know sometimes come in right after work when they have the time. One afternoon you look at your tee-time bookings and see an opening for 3:30-4:30. The light bulb goes off in your head and you quickly send out an e-mail to that group, letting them know you have immediate openings and the first five people to respond with a booking get a discount or a free brat.

EVENTS

Every moment on a golf course is an "event." These are not events like weddings and anniversary parties at the clubhouse, but rather experiences had on the golf course.

- A hole in one
- A golf lesson for a kid (or an adult)
- Father's Day
- The first mow of the season
- The first gr ll of the season

All of these things are experiences, moments, events that evoke an emotional response to your customers and potential customers. When we think of marketing, it all comes back to RMRT (Right Message, Right Time).

We call these micro-moments. Yes, running a golf course is busy and hard. But when someone connects with your course on a deeper level, you will have made a potential customer for life.

TEE-TIME

In a study from the Journal of Applied Social Psychology, researchers found that waiters could increase their tips by 23 percent by the simple act of returning to tables with a second set of mints. So do mints have magic powers? Not exactly but the researchers concluded that the mints created the feeling of a personalized experience among the customers who received them.

Therefore, it was the personalized service received that made them enjoy their experience so much more. Whether your golfers are first-timers at your course or long-time members, the experience matters; online, before they tee off, their round, and their time in the clubhouse.

Make a memorable experience each-and-every time and your marketing will take care of itself.

◀ REFERENCES

1. https://www.forbes.com/sites/jimmyrohampton/2017/05/03/does-social-media-influence-millennials-shopping-decisions/#77a7c22b4cf3
2. https://www.inc.com/jim-schleckser/apple-s-boring-mission-statement-and-what-we-can-learn-from-it.html
3. http://www.ucsusa.org/our-work/center-science-and-democracy/promoting-scientific-integrity/at-nasa-earth-is-removed.html#.WhLFxbQ-eRs
4. https://www.usta.com/en/home/about-usta/who-we-are/national/how-the-usta-works-for-you.html
5. http://www.usga.org/content/usga/home-page/about.html
6. https://www.emarketer.com/Article/US-Adults-Now-Spend-12-Hours-7-Minutes-Day-Consuming-Media/1015775
7. https://www.zenithmedia.com/26-of-media-consumption-will-be-mobile-in-2019/
8. http://trifectaresearch.com/wp-content/uploads/2015/09/Generation-Z-Sample-Trifecta-Research-Deliverable.pdf

www.ingramcontent.com/pod-product-compliance
Lightning Source LLC
Chambersburg PA
CBHW070937220526
45468CB00005B/1806